AMERICA AT WAR

WORLD WAR II
1939-1945

Simon Rose

www.av2books.com

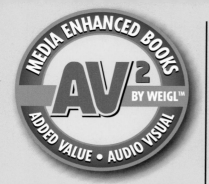

AV² provides enriched content that supplements and complements this bo
Weigl's AV² books strive to create inspired learning and engage young mi
in a total learning experience.

Your AV² Media Enhanced books come alive with...

Audio
Listen to sections of
the book read aloud.

Key Words
Study vocabulary, and
complete a matching
word activity.

Video
Watch informative
video clips.

Quizzes
Test your knowledge.

Embedded Weblinks
Gain additional information
for research.

Slide Show
View images and
captions, and prepare
a presentation.

Try This!
Complete activities and
hands-on experiments.

... and much, much mor

Go to **www.av2books.com,**
and enter this book's
unique code.

BOOK CODE

H303016

AV² by Weigl brings you media
enhanced books that support
active learning.

Published by AV² by Weigl
350 5th Avenue, 59th Floor
New York, NY 10118

Website: www.av2books.com   www.weigl.com
Copyright ©2014 AV² by Weigl

Library of Congress Cataloging-in-Publication Data

Rose, Simon, 1961-
World War II / Simon Rose.
    pages cm. -- (America at war)
Includes index.
ISBN 978-1-62127-659-3 (hardcover : alk. paper) -- ISBN 978-1-62127-660-9 (softcover : alk. paper)
1. World War, 1939-1945--United States--Juvenile literature. I. Title. II. Title: World War Two. III. Title: World War 2.
D769.R64 2013
940.53'73--dc23

                              2013000843

Printed in the United States of America in North Mankato, Minnesota
2 3 4 5 6 7 8 9 0 18 17 16 15 14

122014
WEP151214

Editor: Heather Kissock
Design: Mandy Christianson

Photograph Credits
We acknowledge Getty Images, Alamy, Newscom, and Flickr as our primary photo suppliers.

Every reasonable effort has been made to trace ownership and to obtain permission to reprint copyright material. The publishers would be pleased
to have any errors or omissions brought to their attention so that they may be corrected in subsequent printings.

CONTENTS

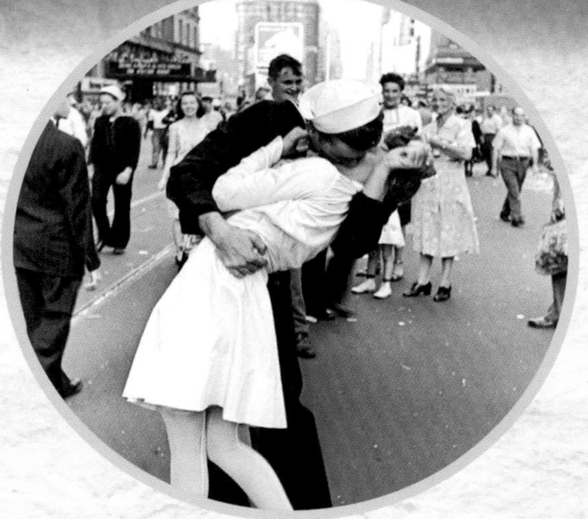

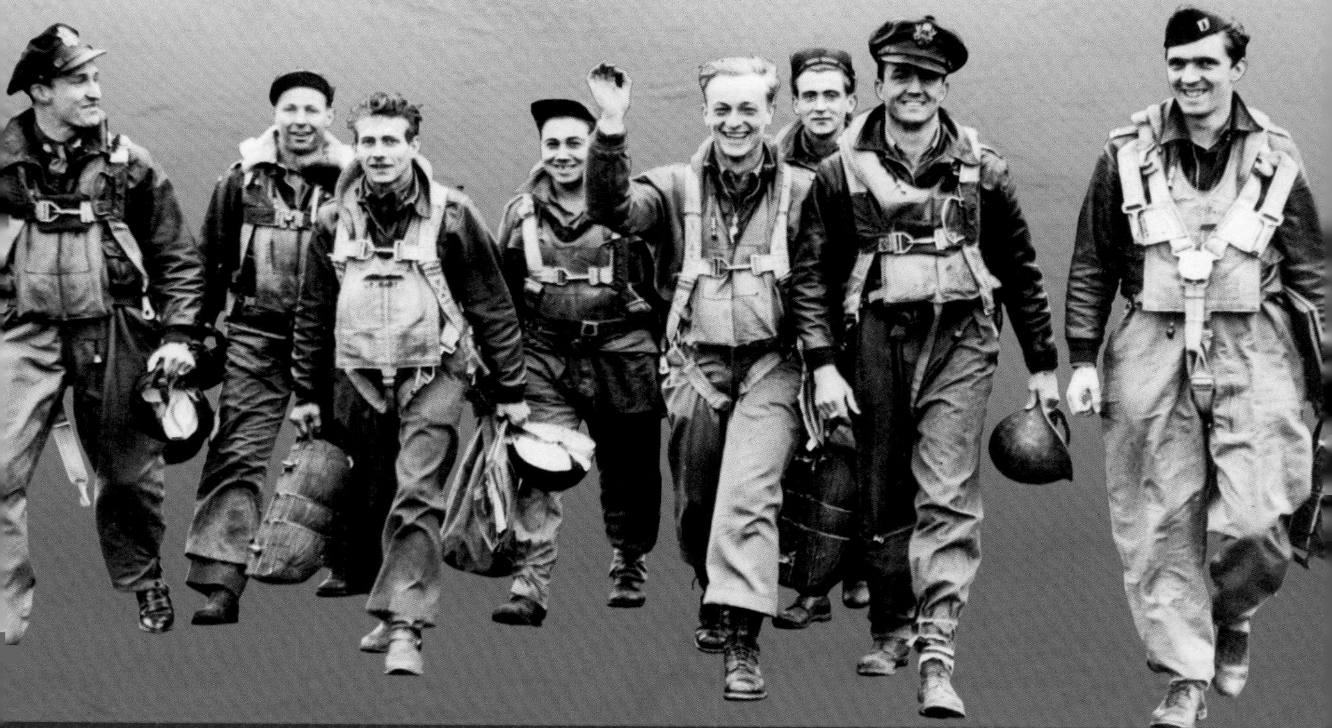

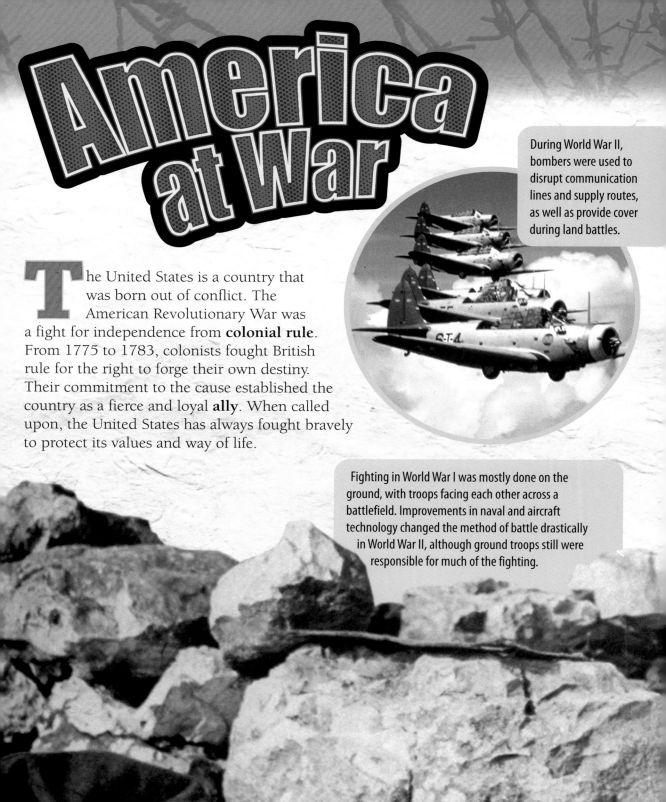

America at War

The United States is a country that was born out of conflict. The American Revolutionary War was a fight for independence from **colonial rule**. From 1775 to 1783, colonists fought British rule for the right to forge their own destiny. Their commitment to the cause established the country as a fierce and loyal **ally**. When called upon, the United States has always fought bravely to protect its values and way of life.

Fighting in World War I was mostly done on the ground, with troops facing each other across a battlefield. Improvements in naval and aircraft technology changed the method of battle drastically in World War II, although ground troops still were responsible for much of the fighting.

Since its inception, the United States has been involved in a number of wars and conflicts. These include the War of 1812, the American Civil War, the Mexican-American War, and several battles with American Indians. The United States was also involved in the latter stages of World War I and played a major role in World War II. Since 1945 alone, the United States has taken part in conflicts in Korea, Vietnam, Iraq, and Afghanistan.

No matter how a war ends, it usually leads to changes for both sides of the conflict. On the global scale, borders change, new countries are created, people win their freedom, and **dictators** are deposed. Changes also occur on a national level for almost every country involved.

The United States has experienced great change as a result of war. War has shaped the country's political, economic, and social landscapes, making it the country it is today.

A War Begins

On September 1, 1939, German troops launched a full-scale invasion of Poland. The attack was waged from land, air, and sea. German tanks began the onslaught, rolling over the Polish border with the **infantry** following close behind. Soon after, bombers entered Polish air space and dropped their cache on the towns below. In the meantime, German ships fired on the Polish navy in the Baltic Sea. More than 1.5 million German troops were involved in the *Blitzkrieg*. Poland had little hope against an attack of this magnitude.

The reasons for the invasion were deeply rooted in the events that ended World War I. The Germans had experienced a humiliating defeat. They were forced into an agreement that reduced the country to a fraction of what it once had been. The resentment over this agreement led to the rise of a new political party and a renewed sense of **nationalism**. The country wanted to return to its former glory.

Word of the invasion of Poland spread quickly throughout Europe. Within days, Great Britain and France, Poland's allies, declared war on Germany. This was the beginning of World War II.

Germany had not formally declared war on Poland when German tanks and troops began their invasion of the country.

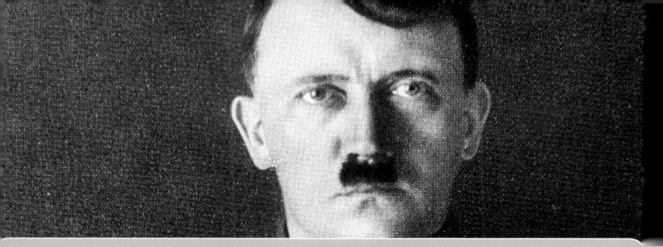

The Roots of World War II

TREATY OF VERSAILLES

Germany had no say in the terms of its surrender at the end of World War I. The **Treaty** of Versailles was presented to German representatives, who were told to sign. In doing so, Germany took full responsibility for initiating the war. It agreed to give up 10 percent of its lands to France and Poland and to decrease the size of its army. Germany also had to pay for repairs to countries affected by the war. These payments, called reparations, severely damaged the German economy. Germans grew angry at what the treaty had done to their country.

THE RISE OF THE NAZIS

German resentment over the Treaty of Versailles led to the rise of Adolf Hitler and the right-wing **Nazi** Party. Hitler took advantage of the frustration people were feeling. He blamed Germany's problems on the treaty and on Jewish and **communist** "traitors." He became **chancellor** of Germany in 1933. In defiance of the treaty, he began to increase the size of Germany's military. He also began to jail anyone who spoke out against the Nazi Party. In 1935, the passage of the Nuremberg Laws began Hitler's persecution and eventual extermination of German Jews.

LEAGUE OF NATIONS

When World War I ended, the **Allied Powers** created the League of Nations to settle international disagreements. The League was weakened, however, when the United States refused to join. Sensing this weakness, Germany formed an alliance with Italy and Japan. Together, these countries became known as the Axis Powers. When the Spanish Civil War erupted in 1936, Germany and Italy sent military aid to Spain's **right-wing** nationalists. The League was unable to stop the conflict in Spain or Italy's subsequent invasion of Ethiopia.

APPEASEMENT

The League of Nations' inability to resolve conflicts led some politicians to seek new ways to maintain peace. France and Great Britain decided on a policy called **appeasement** when dealing with Germany. At its essence, this policy gave Hitler whatever he wanted. When Hitler seized Austria in 1938, France and Great Britain did nothing. When he demanded that the German-speaking areas of Czechoslovakia be handed over, France and Great Britain agreed. It was only when Hitler began his invasion of Poland that he met with resistance.

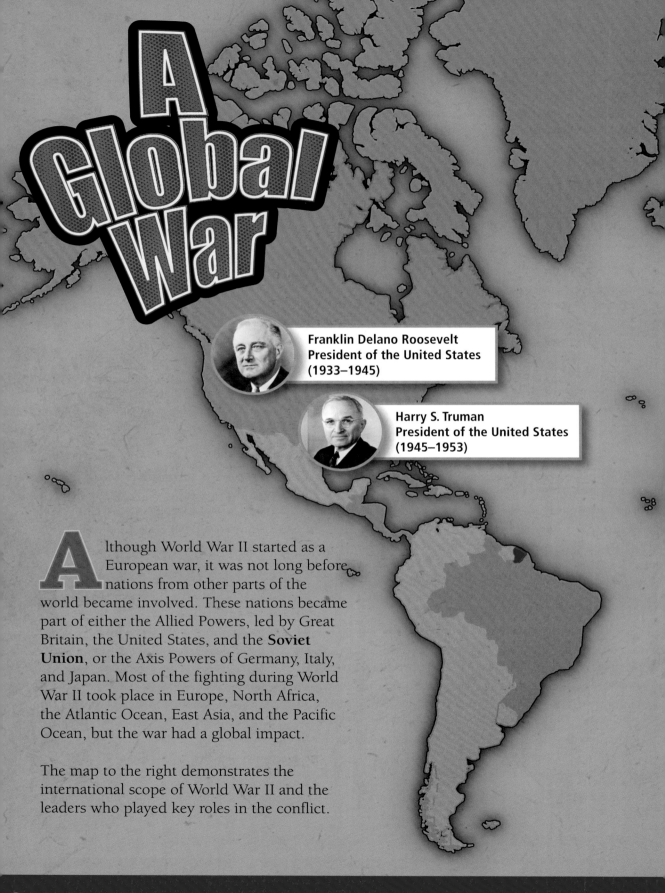

A Global War

Franklin Delano Roosevelt
President of the United States
(1933–1945)

Harry S. Truman
President of the United States
(1945–1953)

Although World War II started as a European war, it was not long before nations from other parts of the world became involved. These nations became part of either the Allied Powers, led by Great Britain, the United States, and the **Soviet Union**, or the Axis Powers of Germany, Italy, and Japan. Most of the fighting during World War II took place in Europe, North Africa, the Atlantic Ocean, East Asia, and the Pacific Ocean, but the war had a global impact.

The map to the right demonstrates the international scope of World War II and the leaders who played key roles in the conflict.

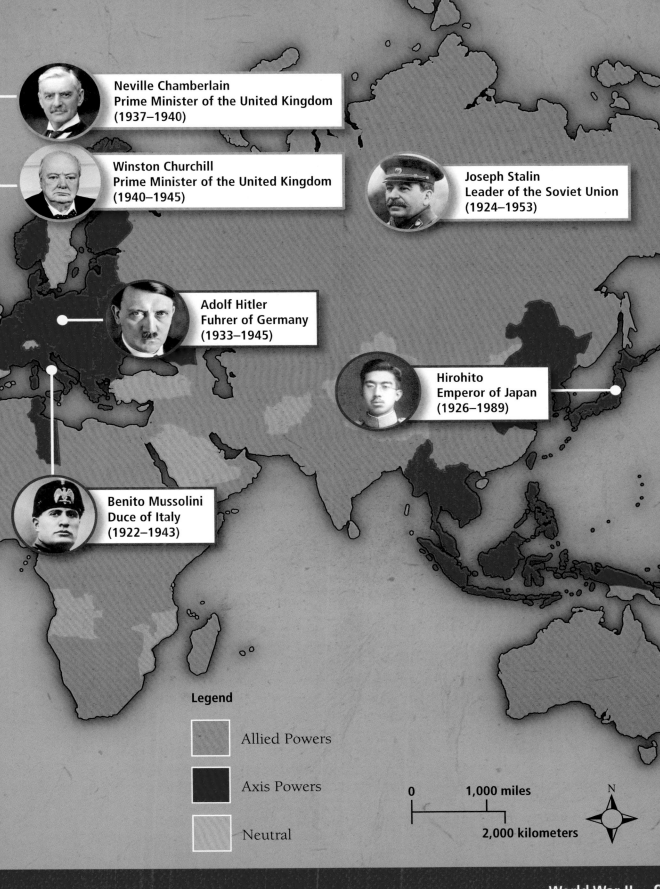

Neville Chamberlain
Prime Minister of the United Kingdom
(1937–1940)

Winston Churchill
Prime Minister of the United Kingdom
(1940–1945)

Joseph Stalin
Leader of the Soviet Union
(1924–1953)

Adolf Hitler
Fuhrer of Germany
(1933–1945)

Hirohito
Emperor of Japan
(1926–1989)

Benito Mussolini
Duce of Italy
(1922–1943)

Legend

Allied Powers

Axis Powers

Neutral

0   1,000 miles

2,000 kilometers

N

The United States Enters the War

Americans were initially reluctant to get involved in Europe's troubles. They remembered the negative effect World War I had on the U.S. economy and the citizens themselves. Despite this opposition, however, President Franklin D. Roosevelt sent Great Britain as much help as he could, without actually declaring war on Germany and Italy. U.S. aid included ships, supplies, and weapons that were often the target of the German **u-boats** operating in the Atlantic Ocean.

The USS *Shaw* was extensively damaged during the attacks on Pearl Harbor. The ship was repaired after several months and served through the remainder of World War II.

The United States was actually more concerned about events that had been occurring in Asia in the years leading up to the war. Japan, in particular, had been forcefully exerting its power over other Asian nations. By the end of 1937, Japan controlled large parts of China and was making motions toward taking control of several European and U.S. possessions in the area.

U.S. leaders were worried about Japanese intentions toward the U.S.-ruled Philippines. They began negotiating with Japan to keep the situation under control. However, in the early morning of December 7, 1941, Japan launched a surprise attack against the U.S. naval base at Pearl Harbor in Hawai'i. The attack by Japanese planes and submarines lasted only two hours, but was still able to inflict severe damage. More than 2,400 Americans were killed, and more than 1,100 wounded. Twenty-one ships were sunk or damaged.

The following day, President Roosevelt made a speech to a joint session of Congress in Washington, D.C. In that speech, he declared the United States to be at war with Japan. When the other Axis Powers joined Japan in its war against the United States, the U.S. government declared war on them as well. The United States was one of the leading members of the Allied Powers.

Franklin D. Roosevelt
The 32ⁿᵈ U.S. President

Franklin Delano Roosevelt was born in New York State in 1882. As a young man, he attended both Harvard University and Columbia University, where he graduated with a law degree. Soon after graduation, he entered political life and was elected to the New York Senate in 1910. He became the state's governor in 1928. Four years later, he was elected president of the United States.

The country was in the throes of the **Great Depression** at the time. To help the United States recover from the economic crisis, Roosevelt introduced a series of programs and reforms known as the New Deal. The plan contributed to his re-election in 1936 and again in 1940. By that time, there was very strong opposition to U.S. involvement in any kind of war. His effective leadership of the United States after the Japanese attack on Pearl Harbor gained him respect within the United States and throughout the world. Roosevelt was elected for a fourth term in 1944, but died in April 1945.

The Great Depression was a time of economic hardship. Many people were out of work and had to rely on soup kitchens for their food.

On December 8, 1941, Franklin D. Roosevelt signed the formal Declaration of War against Japan. He declared war on Italy and Germany three days later.

Americans Who Served in World War II

There were approximately 335,000 people serving in the U.S. military in 1939. By the end of World War II in 1945, that number had increased to more than 12 million. During the war, Americans served in a variety of roles. Military personnel included ground soldiers, sailors, and airmen. People also joined the military's auxiliary services, signing up as doctors, nurses, drivers, cooks, and maintenance crews to provide support for the combat soldiers. Others were enlisted to intercept enemy radio messages and crack German and Japanese codes.

Ground Soldiers

When the United States declared war on Japan, Germany, and Italy, most of its soldiers were in the infantry. Infantry soldiers are troops who fight as ground forces. They march into battlefields carrying little more than their guns, and attack the enemy on foot. Some infantry soldiers have special training. U.S. Marines, for instance, are trained in **amphibious attack**.

Infantry soldiers are often accompanied into the battlefield by artillery units. Artillery soldiers are troops that operate heavy guns, such as tank and anti-aircraft guns. Their job is to fire upon strategic enemy locations and destroy them. Artillery weapons are designed to have a higher impact than those of an infantry soldier.

Soldiers in artillery units underwent extensive training in big gun operation.

Airmen

In World War II, the U.S. Army Air Force and the Navy both operated aircraft. In the Pacific Ocean, planes had few land bases, so they were launched from aircraft carriers. U.S. pilots fought air battles against their Japanese counterparts. They also flew on bombing missions to Japan.

In Europe, the Allies conducted a lengthy bombing campaign against Germany's cities, industries, and military targets. Some pilots often flew as escorts to protect bombers from enemy fighters. Other pilots operated the bombers. A bomber had a crew of about 10 people. Besides the pilot, the crew consisted of the co-pilot, navigator, bombardier, flight engineer, and several different gunners. U.S. bombing missions took place during the day, and **casualties** were often high.

The United States had several flying aces during World War II. Pilots, such as Captain Robert S. Johnson, were known for their ability to shoot down enemy planes.

THE TUSKEGEE AIRMEN

During World War II, black and white Americans were not allowed to serve together in the U.S. military. The 332nd Fighter Group, or Tuskegee Airmen, were the first African American airmen in the U.S. Armed Forces. Members of the 332nd Fighter Group were part of the invasions of North Africa, Sicily, and Italy, and flew over Europe as bomber escorts.

Sailors

The U.S. Navy experienced the first U.S. losses of World War II when the fleet at Pearl Harbor was attacked. It rebuilt quickly, however, and its sailors played key roles in both Europe and Asia.

In Europe, U.S. sailors were part of amphibious operations as they transported men and equipment to the invasion beaches. They also escorted merchant ships in the Atlantic Ocean, making their way to Great Britain with vital supplies. If a German u-boat was detected, U.S. sailors did not hesitate to engage it in battle.

In the Pacific, sailors were important to the operation of U.S. aircraft carriers, where crews were responsible for the maintenance and launching of the planes. Sailors also served on submarines in the Pacific **theater**. U.S. submarines were responsible for more than 30 percent of the Japanese Navy's losses and 60 percent of the losses in Japan's merchant fleet. This greatly affected Japan's ability to continue its war effort, since it could no longer obtain military supplies.

Sailors had to be prepared for various situations that could arise on the ship. They gathered regularly for drills and exercises.

By 1943, the U.S. Navy was larger than the combined fleets of all the other countries fighting in World War II. By the end of the war, the U.S. Navy was operating 6,768 ships.

Women's Army Auxiliary Corps

The Women's Army Auxiliary Corps (WAAC) was founded in 1942, and became the Women's Army Corps (WAC) in 1943. These were the first women other than nurses who were allowed to serve in the army. The WAC performed a variety of non-combat jobs. Some worked in transportation, serving as mechanics, control tower operators, and drivers. Others had jobs at army post offices and hospitals. Many women also worked in communications and clerical positions. As women took over these jobs, more men were released for combat duty. Approximately 150,000 U.S. women served in the WAAC and WAC during World War II. While most served in the United States, some women were sent to work in Europe, Asia, and Africa.

The official reason for establishing the Women's Army Auxiliary Corps was "for the purpose of making available to the national defense the knowledge, skill, and special training of women of the nation."

During World War II, women also served in the Women's Air Service Pilots (WASPs). Female pilots helped the war effort by delivering airplanes, testing planes, and performing flight checks, as well as serving many other tasks.

A Soldier's Uniform

HELMET
The M1 helmet was made of steel with a plastic and fabric liner. It weighed 35 ounces (1 kilogram). The helmet was designed to protect the wearer from shrapnel, but it did not stop bullets. Sometimes, netting was placed over the helmet so that small branches and leaves could be added. This provided the soldier with extra camouflage.

Soldiers heading to war were equipped with a standard uniform that they wore while on active duty in the field. Each soldier also had a kit that accompanied the uniform. The kit contained all the equipment the soldier was expected to need while away from camp. The soldier carried his gear wherever he went. This is an example of the type of uniform worn by U.S. infantry soldiers during World War II.

JACKET
An infantry soldier's jacket was olive drab in color and made of windproof sateen cotton twill. Some jackets came with a detachable hood that could be tucked away if not needed. Ammunition and other small items could be stored in the four front pockets.

TROUSERS
A soldier's trousers were made out of the same material as the uniform jacket. Leggings wrapped around the lower part of the leg and fastened under the shoe.

FOOTWEAR
At the beginning of the war, soldiers wore leather shoes. By late 1943, however, soldiers in Europe were being issued ankle-high combat boots with rubber soles. Specialized boots were also issued to soldiers fighting in tropical or jungle environments.

WEB GEAR

A soldier's web gear was used to carry the supplies needed while away from camp. Web gear consisted of a system of canvas straps, suspenders, belts, and pouches. It was worn over the soldier's uniform, providing easy access to ammunition, food, and first-aid supplies.

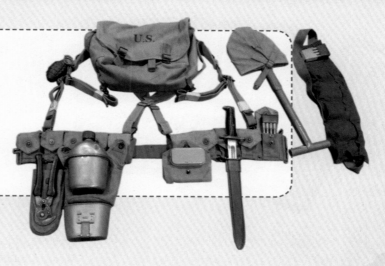

CANTEEN

While out in the field, it was important for a soldier to stay hydrated. All soldiers were issued a canteen in which to carry clean drinking water. Canteens issued during World War II were made of aluminum, stainless steel, porcelain, or plastic. All could hold up to 1 quart (0.95 liters) of water. Soldiers working in tropical climates often carried more than one canteen.

RATIONS

During World War II, U.S. soldiers ate several different types of **rations** while in the field. The C-ration was a pre-cooked, ready-to-eat individual meal. It included a canned meat and vegetable item, and instant coffee. The D-ration was for emergencies and consisted of a high-calorie chocolate bar. K-rations were for specialized assault troops and were designed to provide food for two or three days.

HAVERSACK

Soldiers sometimes attached a haversack, or backpack, to their web gear. The haversack held more supplies than the web gear. This worked well for a soldier who was going to be away from camp for more than a day. A soldier could store a variety of items in the haversack, including extra clothing and ammunition, as well as rations and personal effects.

World War II Weapons

In the years between World War I and II, the U.S. military worked at developing its weaponry. While rifles and other traditional weapons were still used in World War II, several advances in weapons technology allowed troops to have more impact in air, sea, and land battles than in previous wars. Innovation continued throughout the war, leading to weaponry that would change the rules of battle.

GUNS

Most U.S. soldiers were equipped with semiautomatic rifles or submachine guns. However, with tanks taking over the battlefield, soldiers needed a type of gun that could wage war with larger machinery. The bazooka was created as an anti-tank weapon. It fired rockets instead of bullets. Mounted on a soldier's shoulder, the bazooka was used to destroy tanks and enemy field fortifications.

TANKS

The M4 General Sherman tank was the main U.S. Army tank in World War II. The M4 was known for its mobility on the field, due mostly to its small main gun and thin armor. Approximately 50,000 M4 Sherman tanks were built between 1942 and 1945. This number alone made it a formidable force on the battlefields of World War II.

FLAMETHROWERS

Flamethrowers were used extensively by World War II soldiers. These gun-like weapons could send a stream of fire more than 120 feet (37 m) away from the user. Flamethrowers used either gasoline or a gasoline-diesel mixture for fuel. The fuel was kept in canisters that the gunner wore on his back.

AIRCRAFT

World War II involved many large-scale bombing raids. The B-17 Flying Fortress was the key bomber used in U.S. attacks against Germany. The B-17 was known for its durability. Even when severely damaged in battle, it was usually able to return to its airfield. The B-29 Superfortress heavy bomber was one of the largest and most advanced aircraft flown during the conflict. Its remote-controlled machine-gun turrets and electronic fire-control system helped gunners locate their targets faster and fire with more precision. The B-29 was the main aircraft used in the U.S. firebombing campaign against Japan.

AIRCRAFT CARRIERS

Prior to World War II, aircraft carriers performed a support role at sea. They provided air protection and **reconnaissance** for the navy's battleships. As World War II progressed, the military realized that these ships could be used as an **offensive** weapon. As a result, aircraft carriers became the dominant warship used in the Pacific theater. They were used for air raids, carrier-versus-carrier battles, and as amphibious landing support.

THE ATOMIC BOMB

Shrouded in great secrecy, the United States and its allies worked on developing a weapon using the scientific principle of **fission**. Called the Manhattan Project, it involved some of the world's top scientists. The Manhattan Project resulted in the creation of the world's first **atomic bomb**. This weapon alone brought World War II to an abrupt end when the United States used it to attack Japan.

Timeline

The War Overseas

September 1, 1939
Germany invades Poland. Great Britain and France declare war on Germany two days later.

August 25, 1944
U.S. forces help liberate Paris.

December 7, 1941
Japan attacks the U.S. naval base at Pearl Harbor, causing thousands of U.S. casualties. President Roosevelt declares war on Japan the next day.

June 6, 1944
U.S. forces participate in the D-Day invasion on the French coast.

The War at Home

September 16, 1940
The Selective Training and Service Act takes effect, and men are required to enrol for military service.

1942
The government begins rationing by setting limits on the amount of products people can buy.

April 1, 1945
The Americans launch an attack on Okinawa, claiming the island by the end of June.

May 8, 1945
The Germans surrender to the Allied forces.

December 16, 1944 to January 16, 1945
U.S. forces fight the Battle of the Bulge, or Ardennes Offensive, in Belgium. The battle is won, but more than 19,000 U.S. troops die.

February 1945
The Americans attack the Japanese island of Iwo Jima, claiming it as their own a month later.

August 15, 1945
Following the dropping of atomic bombs on Hiroshima and Nagasaki, Japan surrenders to the United States. The war comes to its official end a month later.

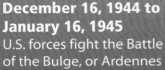

April 1945
President Roosevelt dies and is succeeded in office by Harry Truman.

February 1942
President Roosevelt orders the **internment** of Japanese Americans.

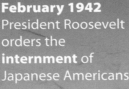

American Battles

When the United States entered World War II, its main battle was perceived to be with Japan. The country's entry into the war was multifaceted, however. It sent its military to almost every part of the world affected by the war. The U.S. Navy dispatched ships, submarines, and planes to the Pacific, where they were soon joined by members of the U.S. Army and Marines. The Army was also sent to fight in North Africa, Italy, and in Western Europe. The U.S. Air Force conducted bombing campaigns over Germany and other parts of Europe. The country's presence in all of the main theaters of war proved its commitment to vanquishing the enemies.

Bad weather resulted in a rough trip across the English Channel. Many troops arrived on the beaches suffering from seasickness.

The D-Day Invasion

The D-Day invasion took place on June 6, 1944. It was the largest amphibious assault in history, and the beginning of a larger attack called the Invasion of Normandy. The goal of the attack was to wrest control of France away from the Germans and free French citizens from German rule.

Germany had conquered France in June 1940 and had occupied the country ever since. The United States and its allies had already liberated North Africa and Italy, but were determined to liberate France as well. If successful, the invasion would give the Allies a foothold in central Europe and allow Allied forces better access to Germany itself.

JUNE 4

Allied troops begin to board ships in Great Britain, in preparation for the voyage across the English Channel to Normandy.

JUNE 5

The Allied fleet, containing more than 5,000 watercraft, begins its crossing of the English Channel. Weather conditions are poor.

Many of the U.S. landings did not hit their mark. The winds and waves had pushed their vessels off course.

In preparation for the D-Day attack, the Allies bombed airfields, railroads, bridges, and roads in northern France to block German access to the coastline. Then, they set to work bringing their troops onto French soil. In the early morning hours of June 6, Allied aircraft dropped approximately 24,000 paratroopers behind enemy lines. These men were given the job of destroying targets and seizing bridges and other strategic locations. Planes then began bombing German positions, while ships fired on the beaches from out at sea. Under the hail of fire, amphibious vehicles began leaving the larger ships, heading for the beaches of France. U.S. troops landed at beaches codenamed Utah and Omaha. After engaging in a day-long battle with the Germans, U.S. forces secured the area, but at a heavy cost. It is estimated that more than 5,000 Americans were killed, wounded, or went missing while fighting to secure the Utah and Omaha beachheads.

More than 150,000 Allied troops, along with tanks and other equipment, had landed in Normandy by the end of D-Day. More troops soon followed. By July, Allied armies had advanced into northern France. Fighting continued in northern France throughout the summer. The Allies liberated Paris on August 25, and by early fall, U.S. forces were advancing to the German frontier.

JUNE 6

Allied paratroopers are dropped behind German lines in the French region of Normandy. By 6:30 am, seaborne forces arrive on the French coast.

JUNE 7

Allied forces begin their advance into northern France. They are soon joined by reinforcements. After three months of fighting, the Allies liberate Paris on August 25.

Battle of the Bulge

By late 1944, it seemed that the war was almost over. The United States and its allies had advanced to the western border of Germany, while the Soviet army closed in on the east. However, Hitler was not yet ready to surrender to the Allied forces. He decided to launch what he hoped would be a decisive counterattack in the west. The German offensive began on December 16, 1944, in the Ardennes Forest of Belgium and Luxembourg.

It was a bitterly cold winter, and the area had experienced significant snowfall. By this stage of the war, the Allies had solid control of the air, but the cloudy winter skies kept the air force grounded. It also made it difficult for the Allies to gauge the scale of the attack. They did not know that the German forces were made up of almost 1,000 tanks and more than 200,000 troops.

During the Battle of the Bulge, the extreme cold made fighting even more difficult. Soldiers had to deal with exposure to the cold temperatures.

The battle began on December 16 with German artillery bombing the Allied line. German tanks then moved forward, advancing more than 12 miles (19 kilometers) on the first day. The fighting went on for more than a month. At first, it looked like the Germans were going to have a major victory. However, the war had exhausted their resources, and they were rapidly running out of fuel for their tanks. If the battle did not come to a quick end, the Germans would not be able to continue their assault on the Allied lines.

December 16

The Germans launch the Ardennes Offensive, or Battle of the Bulge, in the Ardennes Forest of Belgium and Luxembourg.

December 17

After one day of fighting, the Germans have broken into the Allied line and are advancing toward the Meuse River.

On December 23, the weather began to clear, and the Allies were able to launch a major air attack. Allied ground reinforcements also began to arrive. With the increase in manpower, the Allies were able to push the Germans back. As their fuel supplies were running out, many German soldiers had to abandon their tanks anyway. They began to give up on the fight and return, on foot, to Berlin. By January 25, 1945, the Battle of the Bulge was over.

The battle was the largest and bloodiest battle fought by the Americans in World War II. About 500,000 men were involved in the fighting. By the time it was over, the battle had claimed the lives of more than 19,000 U.S. soldiers. Another 47,500 were wounded.

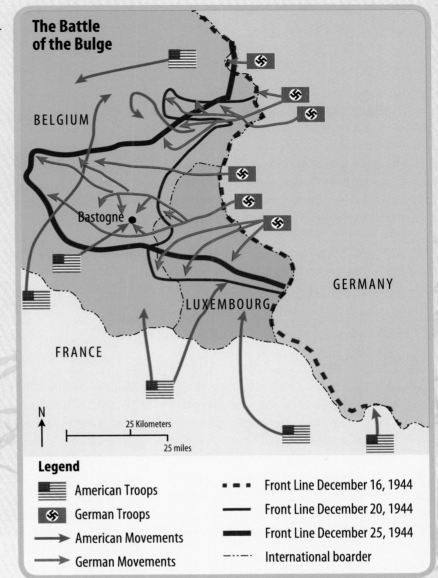

The Battle of the Bulge

BELGIUM

Bastogne

GERMANY

LUXEMBOURG

FRANCE

N

25 Kilometers

25 miles

Legend

American Troops

German Troops

American Movements

German Movements

Front Line December 16, 1944

Front Line December 20, 1944

Front Line December 25, 1944

International boarder

December 23

The skies clear, and the Allied air force begins firing on the German forces. Ground reinforcements also begin arriving to help the Allies drive the Germans back.

January 25

The Battle of the Bulge comes to an end. By March, U.S. forces are able to cross the Rhine into Germany. By May, the Germans have surrendered.

Battle of Okinawa

While the Japanese had the upper hand when the war in the Pacific first started, it was not long before Allied forces began to make their presence known. One by one, they captured islands that were under Japanese control. Finally, the Allies were in sight of the island of Okinawa, located only 340 miles (550 km) south of mainland Japan. The Allied forces wanted to use Okinawa as a base for air operations. The air force would be stationed there to provide support for the planned invasion of the Japanese home islands.

At the time of the attack, Okinawa was defended by more than 130,000 Japanese troops, mostly based in the south part of the island. The soldiers were protected by strong fortifications and defense lines and had orders to fight to the death.

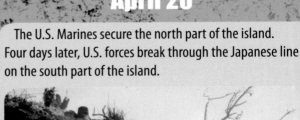

Kamikaze pilots would deliberately crash their aircraft into U.S. ships.

The invasion began on April 1. Approximately 180,000 U.S. Army soldiers and Marines took part in the attack, supported by 300 warships, 1,139 other ships, and several air force units. Within three weeks, the north part of the island was mostly secure.

U.S. forces met heavy resistance in the battle for the south, however. More than 190 **kamikaze** attacks were launched on the U.S. fleet. Even though the Japanese lost many aircraft in these attacks, they were able to cause significant damage to U.S. ships. Over the 82 days of battle, kamikaze attacks led to the sinking of 21 U.S. warships. Another 66 ships were badly damaged.

April 1

With all ships in position, U.S. Army soldiers and Marines land on Okinawa to begin the battle for the island.

April 20

The U.S. Marines secure the north part of the island. Four days later, U.S. forces break through the Japanese line on the south part of the island.

Fighting continued on Okinawa throughout May and June. U.S. army soldiers and Marines had to contend with Japanese forces that had dug themselves into hillsides and caves. They faced constant ambushes and surprise attacks. By the end of June, however, U.S. troops were able to secure the island.

The Battle of Okinawa had the highest number of casualties in the Pacific theater. More than 150,000 Japanese soldiers and local **civilians** were killed, wounded, captured, or committed suicide. There were 49,000 U.S. casualties, including more than 12,000 deaths. Equipment losses were high as well. The U.S. Navy lost 763 aircraft and 36 ships, with another 368 ships damaged. The Japanese lost more than 7,000 aircraft and 16 ships.

The Battle of Okinawa

East China Sea

Bise
Aha
Tako
Nago
OKINAWA
Kurawa
Kin
Hagushi
Chibana
Kuba
Pacific Ocean
Shuri
Itoman

N

5 miles
10 kilometers

Legend

American Troops — American Movements

Japanese Troops — Japanese Movements

— Japanese Front Lines

May 29

In April, the Japanese launch a counterattack to push back U.S. forces. They are unsuccessful. By May 29, the United States has secured the capital city of Naha.

June 21

The island of Okinawa is secured by the U.S. forces. The Japanese general in charge of defending the island commits suicide the next day.

Heroic Americans

The men and women who enlisted for World War II came from a range of backgrounds. They were united by a desire to fight for their country. While all performed heroic acts, as the war progressed, some names became better known than others. Some soldiers were hailed for their bravery and strong leadership. Others were celebrated because they performed feats unlike anyone else.

DWIGHT EISENHOWER
(1890-1969)

Dwight Eisenhower was the supreme commander of Allied Forces in western Europe during World War II. He was responsible for planning the D-Day invasion of Normandy, which led to the liberation of Western Europe.

Eisenhower was born in Denison, Texas, in 1890. He graduated from **West Point** in 1915. After a long career in the army, Eisenhower rose rapidly through the ranks at the beginning of World War II. He led the invasion of French North Africa in November 1942. This led to the Axis surrender of Africa in May 1943. Eisenhower then directed the invasion of Sicily and Italy, which resulted in the fall of Rome in June 1944. The invasion of Normandy occurred soon after.

After the war, Eisenhower remained in the army and became president of Columbia University. He was appointed supreme commander of the North Atlantic Treaty Organization (NATO) in 1951. Two years later, Eisenhower became president of the United States, serving two terms from 1953 to 1961. He published several books after leaving office and died in 1969.

GEORGE S. PATTON
(1885-1945)

George Patton commanded U.S. troops in North Africa, Sicily, and Western Europe. His Third Army captured more enemy prisoners and liberated more territory than any other army in history. Many German commanders regarded Patton as the Allies' best general.

Patton was born in 1885 in San Gabriel, California. He graduated from West Point in 1909 and served in a tank brigade during World War I. Patton's contributions during World War II were considerable. He commanded troops during the U.S. invasion of North Africa in November 1942. He also played a major role in the invasion of Sicily in July 1943. Patton's Third Army arrived in France after the D-Day invasion and proceeded to advance across northern France. After helping to defeat the Germans at the Battle of the Bulge, Patton's forces crossed the Rhine in March 1945. His advance across Germany reached what is now the Czech Republic by the time the war ended in May 1945.

After the war, Patton briefly served as military governor of Bavaria in southern Germany. He died after being severely injured in a car accident in December 1945.

DOUGLAS MACARTHUR
(1880-1964)

Douglas MacArthur commanded the Southwest Pacific Theater in World War II and played a major role in the Allied defeat of Japan.

MacArthur was born in Little Rock, Arkansas, in 1880. He graduated from West Point in 1903. He went on to hold commanding positions during World War I. Between the wars, he was stationed in the Pacific. Over the course of World War II, he staged several offensive campaigns against the Japanese. In 1945, he was appointed commander of all U.S. Army forces in the Pacific. He took charge of the Japanese surrender on September 2, 1945.

After the war, MacArthur became the supreme commander of the Allied Powers in Japan. He later commanded United Nations forces during the early months of the Korean War. He died in Washington in 1964 at the age of 84.

The Home Front

World War II took place far across the Pacific and Atlantic Oceans, but many aspects of U.S. daily life changed while the country was at war. On the home front, Americans endured rationing and shortages of food, fuel, and other supplies, and women entered the workforce in large numbers. People did what they could to contribute to the war effort.

Rationing

The war effort required people to make sacrifices. Many of the items people took for granted were now needed by the troops overseas. Gasoline and other fuels were at a premium, as were certain foods. In 1942, the government began setting limits on the amounts people could purchase of certain items. Families were issued ration stamps so they could buy their allotment of meat, sugar, coffee, butter, cheese, gasoline, tires, clothing, oil, and coal.

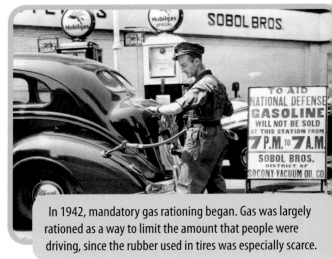

In 1942, mandatory gas rationing began. Gas was largely rationed as a way to limit the amount that people were driving, since the rubber used in tires was especially scarce.

The Draft

On September 16, 1940, the Selective Training and Service Act (STSA) came into effect in the United States. Also known as the draft, this act brought in compulsory military registration for all men between the ages of 21 and 45 years of age. Most Americans supported the draft. Even though the United States had not yet declared war, people believed it was only a matter of time before the United States would be drawn into the conflicts already raging in Europe and East Asia. They wanted their country to be ready to fight.

The draft lottery was attended by reporters and was televised and broadcast throughout the country.

Under the terms of the STSA, men who were selected from the **draft lottery** had to serve in the armed forces for at least one year. As the war progressed, this period of service was extended. By the time the war concluded, 50 million men had registered for the draft, and 10 million had actually joined the armed forces.

Women in the Workforce

Once the United States went to war, the government realized that it would need vast amounts of armaments in order to secure victory. Throughout the war years, factories across the United States were at full capacity making aircraft, tanks, ships, vehicles, guns, bombs, and other materials for the war. However, with 10 million men serving in the military, there was a severe shortage of workers.

As a result, many women were recruited to work in the factories, doing work that had previously been open to men only. Women became electricians, riveters, and welders. They helped build ships, assemble aircraft, and manufacture bombs. Over the course of the war, the United States produced more than 2 million trucks, 300,000 military aircraft, approximately 100,000 tanks and armored vehicles, and thousands of ships. This volume would not have been accomplished without women working in the factories.

Rosie the Riveter was featured in posters and songs throughout World War II. She promoted the idea that women who worked in factories were patriotic.

At the beginning of the war, women made up about one quarter of the workforce, and by the end of the war that amount had increased to one third. About 3 million women worked in factories. However, the majority of the jobs women occupied were administrative in nature.

Japanese Americans

The attack on Pearl Harbor had a significant impact on Japanese Americans. While considered U.S. citizens before the war, they were treated with great suspicion and accused of being spies after Pearl Harbor. Japanese Americans were perceived as a threat to the security of the United States. In February 1942, President Roosevelt signed Executive Order 9066. This new law ordered the removal of Japanese Americans from the West Coast. More than 110,000 Japanese Americans were forcibly removed from their homes and sent to live in internment camps.

People who were as little as 1/16th Japanese, meaning they had only one great great grandparent who was Japanese, could be removed and interned during the wa

Similar to prisons, the internment camps had guards and were surrounded by barbed wire fences. Most of the camps were in very isolated areas and were not suited to family living. People lived in cramped conditions, with limited access to cooking and plumbing facilities. While they were interned, many of their homes were sold, leaving them with nowhere to go upon release. When the war came to an end, Japanese Americans had to start rebuilding their lives.

In 1988, President Ronald Reagan apologized for the Japanese internment on behalf of the U.S. government. More than $1.6 billion was eventually paid to Japanese victims and their families.

Of the 110,000 Japanese Americans interned during World War II, more than half were children. People from within the internment camps were enlisted to educate the children, even though many of them were not qualified teachers.

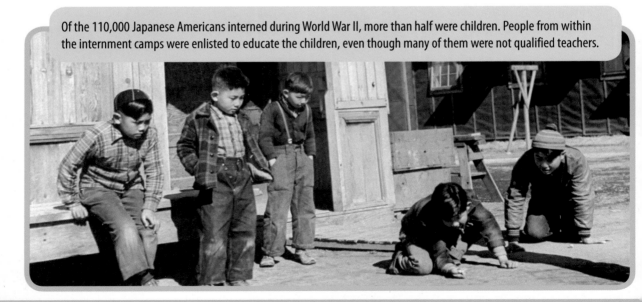

Propaganda

The U.S. government developed many materials designed to promote the country's war effort. Posters were one of the most common forms of **propaganda** used. Some posters served to justify the country's participation in the war. Others drew attention to the flaws of the enemy. The posters were one way for the government to get its message to the U.S. people.

Not all propaganda was generated by the government, however. In the days before television, radio was a main source of news and entertainment for Americans. During the war, patriotic songs with war-related themes were played to encourage pride in the U.S. war effort. Journalists also provided reports on U.S. victories in the Pacific and European theaters.

Hollywood was also very involved in the war effort. Many movies made in the early 1940s had war-related stories. Hitler and the Nazis were portrayed as evil or buffoons, while U.S. characters were always brave and strong. Movie studios worked closely with the U.S. government's Bureau of Motion Picture Affairs to make films that reflected the U.S. perspective.

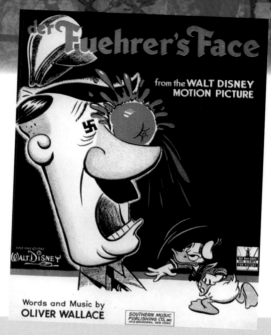

In 1943, Walt Disney released the propaganda film *Der Fuehrer's Face*. Cartoons of several Nazi leaders feature in the film, which went on to win an Academy Award for best animated short film.

Many film stars served during World War II, including Clark Gable. The fact that even Hollywood stars were enlisting in the army helped enforce the idea that everyone should play a part in the war effort.

The War Comes to an End

The entry of the United States into the war was a turning point for the Allies. The Americans brought a renewed energy to a fight that had been losing ground. Between 1942 and 1943, British and U.S. troops defeated the German and Italian forces in North Africa, and invaded Sicily and Italy.

Trying to get control of the eastern **front**, Hitler decided to invade Russia. However, he underestimated the Russian forces. In the winter of 1942–1943, Russia defeated the German forces in the Battle of Stalingrad. During the battle, the Russians took 90,000 prisoners, and the German army began to retreat toward Berlin. By mid-1943, u-boats were losing the battle against sonar equipment and Allied aircraft.

On June 4, 1944, the Allied armies entered Rome. Two days later, D-Day took place on the shores of Normandy. Americans and **Free French** forces liberated Paris in August. It took almost 11 months before western troops met their Soviet Allies near the Elbe River in central Germany.

Following the liberation of Paris, American troops participated in a victory parade that was held along the city's famous Champs-Élysées.

On April 27, 1945, Italy's leader, Benito Mussolini, was captured by his own people and shot the next day. Three days later in his underground bunker, Hitler took his own life. On May 8, 1945, Germany surrendered unconditionally to the Allied forces.

Meanwhile, the U.S. Navy had all but destroyed the Japanese navy and air force. The United States had secured the Japanese island of Iwo Jima in late March. The capture of Okinawa three months later cemented the United States' hold on the Pacific theater. Now in control of two islands within striking range of Japan, the United States was finally in position to attack Japanese cities and pressure Japan to surrender.

The photograph of an American sailor spontaneously kissing a nurse in Times Square following the U. S. victory over Japan became a well-known image from World War II. The picture represented the entire country's excitement when World War II came to an end.

However, Harry Truman, who had become U.S. president following Roosevelt's death in April, knew that an invasion of Japan would involve huge casualties. Truman believed that using the new atomic bombs might help to save U.S. lives. On August 6, an atomic bomb was dropped on the Japanese city of Hiroshima. It is estimated that about 80,000 people died as a result of the bombing, many of them suffering slow, painful deaths from radiation poisoning. Following the attack, the United States demanded that the Japanese surrender. There was no reply. Three days later, the bombing was repeated at Nagasaki. About 40,000 people were incinerated in a nuclear inferno. Japan surrendered unconditionally on August 15, 1945. The war officially came to an end on September 2.

On May 4, 1945, Germany's General Admiral Hans-Georg von Friedeberg signed the surrender of German armed forces in Holland, northwest Germany, and Denmark.

World War II officially came to an end when Japan surrendered. General Yoshijiro Umezu signed the country's unconditional surrender on September 2, 1945, onboard the USS *Missouri*.

The Aftermath

While people all over the world celebrated the end of the war, there were still many outstanding issues. The war had wreaked havoc on the countries involved and their people. The scope of the atrocities against European Jews was only truly realized when the cleanup began. The war had also brought about a severe economic downturn in Europe. To avoid future battles of this scale, politicians searched for solutions.

The United Nations

The League of Nations had been established after World War I to deal with disputes between countries. Even though the League had been unable to prevent aggression in the 1930s, the idea of an international organization was still popular. At the end of World War II, the United Nations was set up to resolve problems through diplomacy and discussion before they led to war. When the organization was officially founded on October 24, 1945, there were 51 members. These included the five permanent members of the UN Security Council—China, France, the Soviet Union, the United Kingdom, and the United States. Over the years, the United Nations has helped to solve international disputes and has organized peacekeeping and humanitarian missions all over the world.

The United Nations is headquartered in New York City. Other subsidiary headquarters are located in Switzerland, Austria, and Kenya.

War Crimes

During the war, the Allies decided that they would bring war criminals to trial after the fighting was over. A number of high-ranking Nazis were put on trial in Nuremburg, Germany. They were charged with war crimes, crimes against peace, crimes against humanity, and conspiracy to commit such crimes. These charges were later expanded to include crimes related to the **Holocaust**. Many were sentenced to death, and some were sent to prison. In East Asia, trials also took place for Japanese leaders. Some were executed, and others received long prison sentences.

In November 1945, just months after the end of the war, the Nuremberg trials began. The war trials were held in the very same city where the Nazi party held its annual rallies.

The Cold War

Even though the United States and Soviet Union had acted as allies during the war, there was always a thread of tension running through the relationship. As a democratic country, the United States had several issues with the communist ideology of the Soviet Union. When the war ended, the tension was displayed openly. Both countries competed with each other to prove their dominance as a superpower. One of the key ways the countries competed was through an arms race. Both countries built up a cache of weapons, including nuclear arms, in order to intimidate the other country. The Soviet Union and the United States both formed groups of allies that would provide support if a conflict occurred. The Soviet Union created the Warsaw Pact with other Eastern European countries. The United States became a founding member of the North Atlantic Treaty Organization (NATO).

The Cold War even extended into space, with both the United States and the Soviet Union racing to put a person on the Moon. On July 20, 1969, the United States' successful *Apollo 11* mission put the first man on the Moon.

The Marshall Plan

World War II left much of Europe in ruins. Countries needed to rebuild, but most were deeply in debt and their economies were in very poor shape. To help Europe recover, U.S. Secretary of State George Marshall created a program known as the Marshall Plan. The plan set aside U.S. funds to help Europe recover from the war. The money was to be used to rebuild damaged areas and to restart Europe's business sector. Between 1948 and 1951, the United States gave $13 billion in aid to countries in Western Europe. The Soviet Union refused aid for itself and its allies in Eastern Europe. The Marshall Plan was very successful in helping Western European countries recover from World War II.

The United States provided foreign aid in the form of food, clothing, and fuel to Europe. Although these provided temporary relief, the Marshall Plan aimed to restore permanent economic stability to Europe.

By The Numbers

Women in the Military

Approximately 350,000 women joined the U.S. Armed Forces during World War II. While the Army received the most enlistees, women could be found in all divisions.

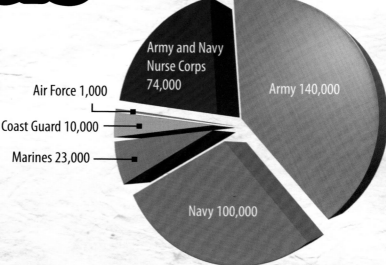

Air Force 1,000

Coast Guard 10,000

Marines 23,000

Army and Navy Nurse Corps 74,000

Army 140,000

Navy 100,000

War Materials

The war had a major impact on U.S. industry. From a Depression era economy at the start of the war, the country increased its output more than 10 times in some industries by 1943.

- Steel
- Rubber
- Aluminum
- Shipbuilding
- Munitions
- Aircraft

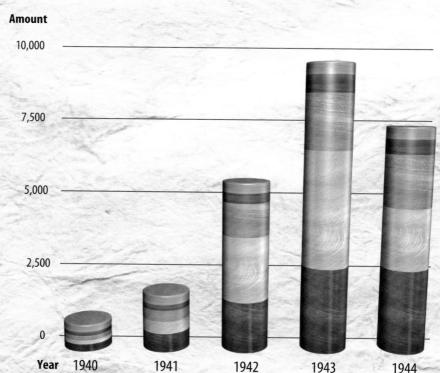

Amount

10,000

7,500

5,000

2,500

0

Year 1940   1941   1942   1943   1944

Women in the Workforce

With the men fighting overseas, women were needed to fill positions in a variety of work sectors. As the war progressed, more women entered the workforce. Some positions were filling jobs men had held. Others were new positions that had been created due to the war effort.

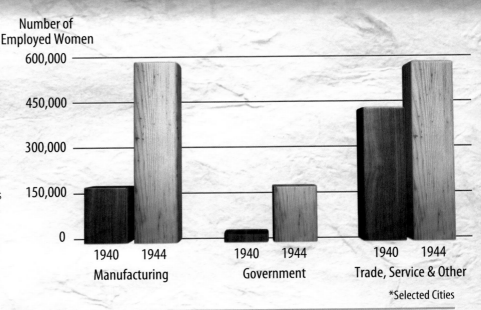

Number of Employed Women

| 600,000 |
| 450,000 |
| 300,000 |
| 150,000 |
| 0 |

| 1940 | 1944 | | 1940 | 1944 | | 1940 | 1944 |
| Manufacturing | | | Government | | | Trade, Service & Other |

*Selected Cities

Tank and Armored Vehicle Production

Even though it came to the war late, the United States quickly became the leader in tank production. Over the course of the war, the Allied forces manufactured more than 225,000 armored vehicles, including tanks. Combined, all of the Axis countries produced only about 50,000.

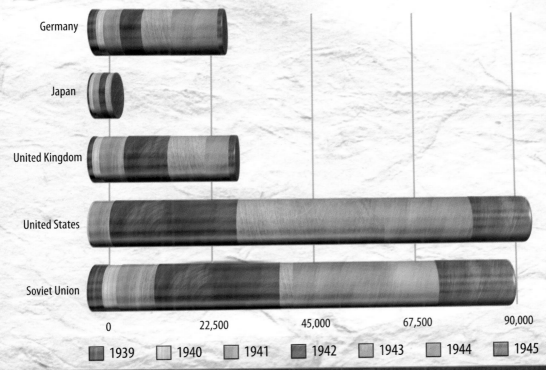

Germany

Japan

United Kingdom

United States

Soviet Union

| 0 | 22,500 | 45,000 | 67,500 | 90,000 |

■ 1939   □ 1940   □ 1941   ■ 1942   □ 1943   ■ 1944   ■ 1945

War Casualties

Calculating the numbers of war dead is difficult. The war led to vast movements of people, some of whom never returned to their homes. Many civilians were caught up in the fighting or died as a result of famine or disease caused by the war. The total number of military deaths, including those who died while prisoners of war, is thought to be around 23 million. Civilian deaths are thought to total at least 34 million and include deaths as a result of bombing, the Holocaust, and Japanese war crimes. These charts show some of the countries that experienced major losses during World War II.

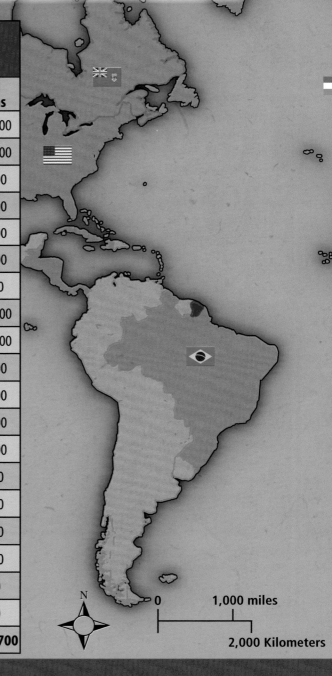

	Country	Military Deaths	Civilian Deaths	Total Deaths
	AXIS POWERS and OCCUPIED AREAS			
	Germany	3,500,000	700,000	4,200,000
	Japan	2,000,000	350,000	2,350,000
	Romania	300,000	160,000	460,000
	Hungary	140,000	290,000	430,000
	Italy	330,000	80,000	410,000
	Austria	230,000	104,000	334,000
	Finland	82,000	2,000	84,000
	Poland	100,000	5,700,000	5,800,000
	Yugoslavia	300,000	1,400,000	1,700,000
	France	250,000	350,000	600,000
	Czechoslovakia	200,000	215,000	415,000
	Netherlands	12,000	198,000	210,000
	Greece	20,000	140,000	160,000
	Belgium	12,000	76,000	88,000
	Albania	28,000	2,000	30,000
	Bulgaria	10,000	10,000	20,000
	Norway	6,400	3,900	10,300
	Luxembourg	5,000	0	5,000
	Denmark	400	1,000	1,400
	Axis Total	**7,525,800**	**9,781,900**	**17,307,700**

N

0   1,000 miles

2,000 Kilometers

ALLIED POWERS

	Country	Military Deaths	Civilian Deaths	Total Deaths
	Soviet Union	10,000,000	10,000,000	20,000,000
	China	2,500,000	7,500,000	10,000,000
	United States	400,000	0	400,000
	United Kingdom	326,000	62,000	388,000
	Canada	45,300	0	45,300
	India	24,000	13,000	37,000
	Australia	23,000	12,000	35,000
	South Africa	7,000	0	7,000
	Ethiopia	5,000	0	5,000
	Brazil	1,000	0	1,000
	Malta	0	2,000	2,000
	Allied Total	**13,331,300**	**17,589,000**	**30,920,300**

How We Remember

At least 400,000 Americans were killed as a result of World War II, with another 270,000 returning home wounded. The bravery of America's military affected everyone in the country. People wanted to honor those who had fought, those who had been injured, and those who had died.

NATIONAL WORLD WAR II MEMORIAL

The National World War II Memorial is located in Washington, D.C. The memorial honors the 16 million people who served in the U.S. Armed Forces during the war, as well as those who died and those who supported the war effort on the home front.

The memorial has 56 pillars and two arches surrounding a fountain and plaza. The Freedom Wall features 4,048 gold stars. Each of these stars represents 100 Americans who were either killed in World War II or remain missing. The memorial opened in 2004, and millions of people visit the site each year.

USS *ARIZONA* MEMORIAL

The USS *Arizona* Memorial is located in Pearl Harbor, Hawai'i. Situated above the sunken wreck of the USS *Arizona*, it is the final resting place of many of the 1,177 crew members killed in the Japanese attack on December 7, 1941.

In 1999, the USS *Missouri* was moved to Pearl Harbor and docked near the memorial. Locating the two ships at Pearl Harbor symbolizes the beginning and end of the United States' participation in World War II.

NORMANDY AMERICAN CEMETERY AND MEMORIAL

The Normandy American Cemetery and Memorial is the final burial place for many of the Americans who died during the D-Day invasion. Located near Omaha Beach, it contains the graves of almost 10,000 troops.

The memorial features a series of columns arranged in a semicircle. Maps and descriptions of the battle are found at each end of the semicircle. A sculpture called *The Spirit of American Youth Rising from the Waves* stands in the center of the semicircle. Walls near the sculpture list those men whose bodies were never recovered.

Memorials and other symbols of remembrance began to appear across the country. Some were local monuments, developed by individual communities. Others were created on behalf of the entire country. Today, these memorials and symbols continue to pay tribute to those who served in World War II.

ARDENNES AMERICAN CEMETERY AND MEMORIAL

The Ardennes American Cemetery and Memorial is located in Belgium, near the site of the Battle of the Bulge. More than 5,000 U.S. soldiers are buried here. Most of them died in the Battle of the Bulge.

The focal point of the memorial is a rectangular limestone building that sits atop a stepped platform. The building is adorned with a sculpture of a 17-foot (5.2-m) high American bald eagle and figures representing Justice, Liberty, and Truth. Inside the structure is a small chapel and a series of maps and displays describing aspects of the battle.

WORLD WAR II MEMORIAL TO THE MISSING

Located along the Pacific Coast near San Francisco, California, the World War II Memorial to the Missing pays tribute to the men and women who never returned from the battles of the Pacific theater.

The memorial features a curved granite wall that is engraved with the names of the 412 men and women who were lost or buried at sea during the Pacific conflict. Standing in front of the wall is a sculpture of Columbia, a female figure that represents the United States.

MARINE CORPS WAR MEMORIAL

The Marine Corps War Memorial, in Arlington, Virginia, is also known as the Iwo Jima memorial. It is dedicated to all U.S. Marines who have lost their lives serving their country since 1775. However, the large bronze statue on the memorial is based on one of the best-known photographs of World War II. The statue depicts five Marines and a Navy corpsman raising the U.S. flag on Mount Suribachi on the island of Iwo Jima. Each Marine is about 32 feet (10.7 m) tall, with the entire sculpture reaching a height of 78 feet (23.8 m). The sculpture's flag flies 24 hours a day, seven days a week.

Test Yourself

MIX 'n MATCH

1. Flying Fortress
2. Chancellor of Germany
3. Largest U.S. battle of World War II
4. USS *Arizona* Memorial
5. Tuskegee Airman
6. Executive Order 9066
7. President of the United States 1945 to 1953

a. Harry Truman

b. Japanese internment

c. Pearl Harbor, Hawai'i

d. Battle of the Bulge

e. 332nd Fight Group

f. Adolf Hitler

g. Bomber aircraft

TRUE OR FALSE

1. During World War II, the Axis Powers made more weapons than the Allies.

2. Many celebrities and movie actors joined the armed forces.

3. The M1 helmet protected a soldier from bullets.

4. In 1945, there were 12 million people in the U.S. Armed Forces.

5. The Battle of the Bulge took place near the River Bulge in Belgium.

6. Rosie the Riveter was featured on posters and in songs.

7. The first atomic bomb was dropped on the city of Nagasaki.

8. The Marine Corps War Memorial statue is based on a photograph taken during the Battle of Iwo Jima.

MULTIPLE CHOICE

1. When did the U.S. enter World War II?
   a. September 1, 1939
   b. June 25, 1940
   c. December 8, 1941
   d. November 11, 1942

2. Who were the three main Allied Powers?
   a. United States, Soviet Union, and Italy
   b. United States, Great Britain, and the Soviet Union
   c. Germany, Italy, and Japan
   d. United States, France, and Great Britain

3. How many Japanese Americans were interned during World War II?
   a. 110,000
   b. 45,000
   c. 250,000
   d. 18,000

4. What was the name of one of the beaches attacked by U.S. forces on D-Day?
   a. Gold
   b. Juno
   c. Sword
   d. Omaha

5. Who was the Supreme Commander of Allied Forces in Europe?
   a. Douglas MacArthur
   b. George Patton
   c. Dwight Eisenhower
   d. Chester Nimitz

6. What were ration stamps used for?
   a. Sending items to soldiers at the front
   b. Allowing people to buy only a limited amount of certain products
   c. Forcing people to buy only certain products
   d. Soldiers received them as a reward for bravery

7. On which ship was the Japanese surrender document signed?
   a. USS *Missouri*
   b. USS *Enterprise*
   c. USS *Arizona*
   d. USS *Yorktown*

Key Words

Allied Powers: the countries opposed to Germany, Japan, and Italy during World War II

ally: a person or group who is associated with another for a common purpose

amphibious attack: a military attack that combines land and sea forces

appeasement: the policy of Britain and France to try to accommodate Hitler's demands in the late 1930s without going to war

atomic bomb: a weapon of enormous destructive power, derived from nuclear reactions

blitzkrieg: a swift, sudden military offensive

casualties: people who have been killed, wounded, taken prisoner, or gone missing in action

chancellor: the head of government of some countries

civilians: people who are not members of the military

colonial rule: areas that are under the control of another country

communist: in theory, a system where all people enjoy equal social and economic status

dictators: people who rule absolutely and oppressively

draft lottery: the system used to conscript people into the U.S. military

fission: the splitting of an atomic nucleus into approximately equal parts

Free French: a French movement during World War II that was organized to fight for the liberation of France from Germany

front: the area where armies face each other

Great Depression: a severe worldwide economic slowdown in the decade preceding World War II

Holocaust: a term used to describe the murder of 6 million Jewish and other people during World War II

infantry: ground soldiers

internment: confinement during wartime

kamikaze: the suicide pilots of the Japanese Air Force

nationalism: devoted to the interests of their own country

Nazi: the National Socialist German Workers Party, which ruled Germany from 1933 to 1945

offensive: an attack launched by military forces against the enemy

propaganda: information deliberately spread to help or harm a person, group, or nation

rations: food issued to members of a group

reconnaissance: exploratory survey of an area

right-wing: people that support the preservation of social order

Soviet Union: a large country in eastern Europe and northern Asia from 1922 to 1991, comprising Russia and 14 other republics. Most of the territory is now known as Russia.

theater: the entire land, sea, and air area directly involved in war operations

treaty: an agreement between two or more countries

u-boats: the name given to German submarines

West Point: the United States Military Academy in New York

Index

Log on to www.av2books.com

AV² by Weigl brings you media enhanced books that support active learning. Go to www.av2books.com, and enter the special code found on page 2 of this book. You will gain access to enriched and enhanced content that supplements and complements this book. Content includes video, audio, weblinks, quizzes, a slide show, and activities.

AV² Online Navigation

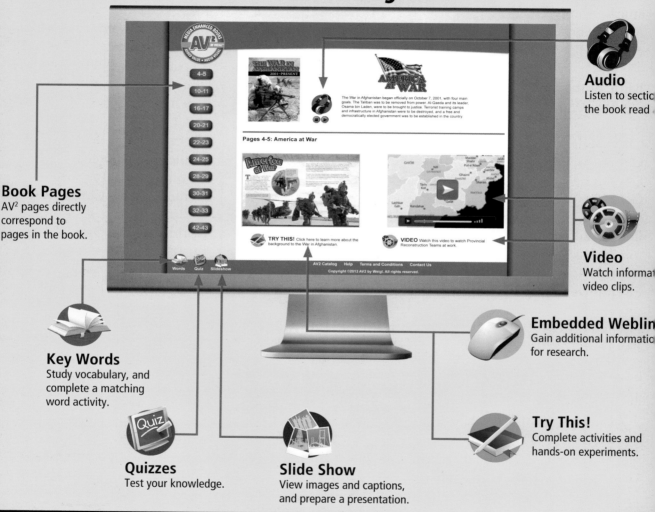

Book Pages
AV² pages directly correspond to pages in the book.

Audio
Listen to secti the book read

Video
Watch informa video clips.

Key Words
Study vocabulary, and complete a matching word activity.

Embedded Weblin
Gain additional informatio for research.

Quizzes
Test your knowledge.

Slide Show
View images and captions, and prepare a presentation.

Try This!
Complete activities and hands-on experiments.

AV² was built to bridge the gap between print and digital. We encourage you to tell us what you like and what you want to see in the future.

Sign up to be an AV² Ambassador at www.av2books.com/ambassador.